Why Aren't We Casting Out Demons?

Why Aren't We Casting Out Demons?

An Honest Question for Christians in the Pulpit and the Pew

Carolyn Walker

Edited by
Donna Scuderi

Without limiting the rights under copyright(s) reserved below, no part of this publication may be reproduced, stored in or introduced into a retrieval system, or transmitted, in any form, or by any means (electronic, mechanical, photocopying, recording, or otherwise) without the prior permission of the publisher and the copyright owner.

The content of this book is provided "AS IS." The Publisher and the Author make no guarantees or warranties as to the accuracy, adequacy or completeness of or results to be obtained from using the content of this book, including any information that can be accessed through hyperlinks or otherwise, and expressly disclaim any warranty expressed or implied, including but not limited to implied warranties of merchantability or fitness for a particular purpose. This limitation of liability shall apply to any claim or cause whatsoever whether such claim or cause arises in contract, tort, or otherwise. In short, you, the reader, are responsible for your choices and the results they bring.

The scanning, uploading, and distributing of this book via the internet or ~~via~~ any other means without the permission of the publisher and copyright owner is illegal and punishable by law. Please purchase only authorized copies, and do not participate in or encourage piracy of copyrighted materials. Your support of the author's rights is appreciated.

Unless otherwise specified, all Scripture quotations are taken from the New King James Version®. Copyright © 1982 by Thomas Nelson. Used by permission. All rights reserved.

All emphasis in Scripture quotations is the author's own.

Copyright © 2024 by Carolyn Walker. All rights reserved.

Released: September 2024 ISBN: 978-1-64457-764-6

Rise UP Publications
www.riseUPpublications.com
Phone: 866-846-5123

To my son, Tiweh White and my daughter, Twannia Clark.

Introduction

Why aren't we casting out demons? This question should resonate deeply within the heart of every Christian, whether standing in the pulpit or worshiping in the pew. This book aims to relieve the unnecessary suffering of the untold numbers held hostage by ignorance surrounding this issue. I want Christians to arise in their God-ordained authority, bring deliverance to the suffering, and deal a mighty blow to the enemy.

Demonic spirits are actively assaulting people's bodies, hindering their progress, and establishing dominion within them. Yet, why are these evil forces seemingly getting away with it? When we encounter demons, we have the authority, in Jesus' name, to command them to leave, and they must obey. However, despite this divine authority, many believers—even church lead-

Introduction

ers—appear unprepared, hesitant, or unwilling to confront demonic manifestations. This begs the question: Why aren't more pastors casting out demons?

Casting out demons has become an unpopular and often neglected aspect of modern Christianity. Despite being a pastor in several churches—including two megachurches—I have seldom witnessed or heard of congregations actively teaching or practicing demon deliverance. Most pastors avoid it altogether, or they offer weak, unscriptural prayers when faced with a manifesting demon. Many are ignorant of the Word of God, unclean in their lifestyles, or afraid of the potential backlash and embarrassment during a church service.

Some pastors have an unrighteous fear that deliverance might negatively impact attendance and negatively impact financial contributions. Other pastors even believe that demonic possession is a problem exclusive to foreign, impoverished countries and not something that affects Christians in America. Such fears and misconceptions highlight the urgent need for this book.

I've witnessed and personally endured the attacks of wicked spirits. I've experienced open visions, horrific nightmares, and even physical manifestations such as unexplainable scratches and cuts on my body. On numerous occasions, I saw dark figures leaving my

Introduction

body and room. Despite these terrifying encounters, the church leaders from whom I sought help lacked the knowledge or courage to help me. This lack of spiritual understanding prompted me to dig deeper into God's Word and seek His divine instructions. Whether casting out demons, healing the sick, or leading someone to salvation, everything must be done according to the Bible.

I pray that this book will incite more Christians—especially leaders—to acknowledge the pervasive work of demonic spirits. This is crucial because we will inevitably encounter these spirits, and we must confront them—not in our strength, but with the power and authority granted by Jesus Christ. Without deliverance from demonic oppression, believers cannot serve God to their fullest potential. Some might even risk forfeiting their place in the Kingdom of God.

This book is a call to action for all Christians to embrace the authority given by Jesus Christ and confront the demonic forces that seek to kill, steal, and destroy. By doing so, we unleash the transformative power of deliverance in our lives, families, churches, communities, and nations. This is not just a challenge but a divine mandate that we must heed for the sake of the Kingdom of God.

Chapter One

Church: Why We Attend and What We Expect

Week in and week out, Christians around the world attend church services. Therefore, it is important to recognize the purpose of our gatherings, our expectations in attending, and our responsibility to respond to demonic disruptions.

The writer of the Book of Hebrews stressed the importance of our gatherings, writing, "Let us consider one another in order to stir up love and good works, not forsaking the assembling of ourselves together, as is the manner of some, but exhorting one another, and so much the more as you see the Day approaching" (Hebrews 10:24–25). At church, we believers can unite in our worship to God. We also have fellowship with one another and deepen our individual and collective understanding of the faith. Our meetings affect us spiritually, physically, and mentally. They foster our growth and increase our knowledge and experience of God. Through sermons, teachings, and Scripture reading, we receive guidance that deepens our relationship with Him, helps us apply His teachings, and enables us to understand ourselves, our strengths, and our struggles more fully.

The Scriptures stress various aspects of our gatherings and help us to understand God's purpose in bringing us together:

- Where two or three are gathered together in My name, I am there in the midst of them (Matthew 18:20).
- Let the word of Christ dwell in you richly in all wisdom, teaching and admonishing one another in psalms and hymns and spiritual songs, singing with grace in your hearts to the Lord (Colossians 3:16).
- He Himself gave some to be apostles, some prophets, some evangelists, and some pastors and teachers, for the equipping of the saints for the work of ministry, for the edifying of the body of Christ, till we all come to the unity of the faith and of the knowledge of the Son of God, to a perfect man, to the measure of the stature of the fullness of Christ (Ephesians 4:11–13).

It is essential that we gather together. Therefore, it is important for church leaders to establish an environment that is conducive to worship and to spiritual growth.

What We Can Expect

Every church is unique but coming together each week (or every few days in some churches) is central to the spiritual growth and health of the local body. We expect church to be a welcoming place for people from all walks of life, cultures, races, and all social classes. We are encouraged to extend invitations to nonbelievers, newcomers, and those seeking a deeper spiritual connection with God and others. All of this is meant to happen in an environment of acceptance and hospitality.

In a safe, inclusive setting, all believers can reflect on their actions and attitudes. This self-examination fosters a spirit of humility and repentance, and it invites nonbelievers to confess, repent, and accept Jesus Christ as their Lord and Savior. Church services are also special sources of renewal and encouragement where praise, worship, and the sharing of testimonials bring solace and the assurance that no one is alone in the journey. This shared experience strengthens bonds among the people, unifying the body of Christ.

Gathered believers are also empowered to live their faith in practical ways. Church services give us the tools we need to serve God and others. The various aspects of our meetings renew our mission to carry the gospel to the entire world. We remember Jesus' Great Commission: "Go therefore and make disciples of all the nations, baptizing them in the name of the Father and of the Son and of the Holy Spirit" (Matthew 28:19). Being in church together develops us as ambassadors of Christ's love and sends us forth to share God's transforming power through faith.

In simple terms, the purpose of our gatherings and our expectations of Christian church services revolve around worshipping God, building relationships with other believers, growing spiritually in God's Word, and serving God and others through His love. When we attend a church service, we can expect the Spirit of God to ignite and nurture our souls. We can see the relationship between God and His creation strengthened. And we can be both equipped and empowered to navigate life's challenges.

Being in church together develops us as ambassadors of Christ's love and sends us forth to share God's transformational power through faith.

Chapter Two

A Pastor's Unwavering Commitment

In the heart of a Christian community, the pastor stands as a guiding light leading the congregation toward spiritual growth, unity, and connection in the Spirit of God. During church services, the pastor's role reaches beyond the pulpit, impacting and shaping the people's experience in worshipping together. The pastor's role is demanding and sometimes thankless. Everything the pastor does, says, or doesn't do draws attention and has an impact. We cannot pray for our pastors enough. And as we pray, let's remember that pastors are human. The only perfect shepherd is the Good Shepherd, Jesus Christ.

Committed to the Church's Well-Being

Whether in or out of the pulpit, the pastor expresses a deep commitment to the well-being of the church and its members. Driving this commitment are the pastor's deep love for God and His people and a genuine concern for the congregation's spiritual, emotional, and physical needs. Just as a shepherd tends to the flock, pastors nurture the individuals entrusted to their care and guidance.

The pastoral commitment to the church's well-being includes the creating of a safe and nurturing spiritual and physical environment in which to gather and worship. In part this means cultivating a Holy Ghost-filled atmosphere in which diverse people from differing backgrounds can come together to freely experience God's presence, grace, and mercy.

The pastor embodies spiritual leadership by faithfully acting according to the calling. For the well-led flock, this means there will be more opportunities to grow, thrive, and be transformed by God's love. The pastor's role far exceeds the leading of services and the preaching of sermons. Pastors are called into the fullness of the Great Commission of Jesus Christ.

What Pastors Do

Pastors provide guidance and encouragement through their sermons, teachings, and interactions, especially within their congregations. They address relevant issues and offer insights from the Scriptures. They can share practical advice that helps members navigate personal challenges and the leading of the Holy Spirit.

Pastors don't only speak; they also listen as people express their fears and concerns. As leaders with first-hand experience of the human condition, they can provide emotional support to those who are facing difficulties. As they open themselves to these relationships and come alongside members of their congregations, pastors create a sense of belonging and a support network that strengthens the community.

Through prayer, fasting, and a consecrated lifestyle, pastors are empowered and equipped to promote spiritual growth and virtues such as compassion, humility, and integrity. Pastors model these virtues by embodying them. The pastor also sets an example for the congregation by encouraging an environment of holiness and then protecting that environment. Sometimes, the pastor does this by managing unexpected disruptions, including demonic manifestations.

Creating a conducive spiritual atmosphere is crucial for worship and fellowship. Disruptive spirits can hinder the congregation's communion with God and one another. Demonic manifestations not only interfere with the people's worship and attention, but they also point out spiritual needs within the local body. When these manifestations erupt, leaders can protect the spiritual environment and well-being of believers by casting out demons whenever they show up.

Many pastors see addressing demonic disruptions as part of their responsibility. Other pastors are not so sure, as we will see in Chapter 6. In this regard, I would simply repeat the words Jesus spoke when He sent out the Twelve: He said, "As you go, preach, saying, 'The kingdom of heaven is at hand'" (Matthew 10:7).

In other words, all believers, and especially those who are responsible for the flock, are called to declare God's kingdom and its preeminence over all other kingdoms. Shrinking back from this call is a form of passively submitting to demonic and satanic incursions and their effects on the church. This undermines God's intent and is antithetical to the pastor's unwavering commitment to God and His people.

The pastor's role is demanding and often thankless. Everything the pastor does, says, or doesn't do draws attention and has an impact. We cannot pray for our pastors enough. And as we pray, let's remember that pastors are human. The only perfect shepherd is the Good Shepherd, Jesus Christ.

Chapter Three

Unmasking Demonic Forces

The devil is a thief. John 10:10 says, "The thief does not come except to steal, and to kill, and to destroy." Satan and his demonic forces gladly do all of that in the hopes of leading people away from their faith in God. This fits into Satan's larger plan, which is to oppose the redemptive work of Jesus Christ.

Many Christian leaders have taught that demons are fallen angels who rebelled against God's authority and joined the kingdom of Satan,[1] who is often referred to as *Lucifer* or *the devil*. Because of their pride and rebellion, God cast Satan and his fallen angels out of heaven. They remain prideful and antagonistic toward God and His people, with a nature characterized by deceit, hatred, and a relentless opposition to God's purposes.

Demonic forces work tirelessly. Their chief aims are to (1) discredit God's authority, (2) lead humanity away from the paths of righteousness, and (3) disrupt all harmony in the relationship between God and His creation.

Demon Characteristics

Demons are not ignorant of God's existence or power. Nor are they aimless or prone to acting randomly. They are not omniscient (as God is), but they know enough to be effective—especially when we are ignorant of them. Therefore, we need to understand demons and the characteristics that they share:

- Demons believe who God is: In his letter to the church, James wrote, "You believe that there is one God. You do well. Even the demons believe—and tremble!" (James 2:19).
- Demons are knowledgeable: When Jesus taught in the synagogue at Capernaum, a demonized man cried out to Him, saying, "Let us alone! What have we to do with You, Jesus of Nazareth? Did You come to destroy us? I know who You are—the Holy One of God!" (Mark 1:24).
- Demons are self-aware: When Jesus asked the demoniac, "What is your name?" (Mark 5:9), "he answered, saying, 'My name is Legion;

for we [demons within] are many'" (Mark 5:9).
- Demons are on the prowl: In his first epistle, Peter warned us, "Be sober, be vigilant; because your adversary the devil walks about like a roaring lion, seeking whom he may devour" (1 Peter 5:8).
- Demons are determined to complete their work: "Then [the unclean spirit] says, 'I will return to my house from which I came.' And when he comes, he finds it empty, swept, and put in order. Then he goes and takes with him seven other spirits more wicked than himself, and they enter and dwell there; and the last state of that man is worse than the first." (Matthew 12:44–45).

How Demons Work

Unclean, evil, wicked, seducing, and familiar disembodied spirits are tasked to negatively influence human lives. They try to prevent individuals from experiencing the grace, mercy, and transformation that are available because of Jesus' sacrifice on the cross. Demons exert their influence by tempting people toward sinful thoughts and behaviors, using subtle suggestions or more overt attempts to distract or manipulate. They also work to promote division, create confusion, and hinder Christian church services.

Demons are crafty. They distort the truth, pervert our perceptions, and support diversions that can lead us astray from God and His Word. Demonic forces also seek to mentally control people while leading them toward destructive thoughts that can eventually bring about their demise.

Demonic forces also stir hateful intentions, bringing individual and collective harm that is not only spiritual but also emotional and physical. Their actions are not haphazard. They have a deep-seated hatred for God and His creation. It inspires them and encourages their persistence in finishing what they start. That is why Peter told us to be "sober and vigilant" (1 Peter 5:8).

Although the devil might strut "like a roaring lion" (1 Peter 5:8), all power and authority within the spiritual realm belong to Jesus Christ, who empowered and equipped believers to defeat the enemy's tactics.

Types of Demonic Spirits

For the record, this is not a book about demonology. It is about (1) recognizing that demons exist and are active, and (2) knowing that Jesus gave us authority to liberate people who are demonically attacked. The following list of demonic spirits and their specialties is not comprehensive, but it provides a sense of the beings at work in certain demonic situations.

- **Incubus:** This demon causes nightmares and has sexual intercourse with women (Genesis 6:2).[2]
- **Succubus:** This female demon has sexual intercourse with men in their sleep and also opens the door to masturbation and homosexuality (Genesis 6:2).[3]
- **Rabshakeh:**[4] This demon releases fear and discouragement that comes to question God as a Christian's source. Additionally, it focuses on whom you are not and what you cannot do (2 Kings 18:17–23).
- **Python:** This demon has snake-like traits; it is not poisonous but squeezes the life out of its victims (Act 16:16–18).
- **Pharmakeia spirit (medication by magic):** In ~~the~~ Greek, the word for "sorcery" is *pharmakeia*.[5] Pharmakeia is also a demon of prescription drugs and recreational drugs such as cocaine.
- **Behemoth:** This demonic spirit generally operates in men as a king of pride and walks hand in hand with Leviathan. It is very strong, greedy, and gluttonous (Job 40:15–24).[6]

- **Lilith:** This female demon/night demon attacks and kills newborn babies and dwells in desolate places.[7] (Lilith appears in the Hebrew and is translated as "night creature" in the NKJV of Isaiah 34:14.)

Demons are knowledgeable, self-aware, and aware of God. In Christ, we are equipped to be knowledgeable, self-aware, and God-aware. Therefore, we can recognize and unmask demonic forces and arrest enemy infiltrators, for the sake of the body of Christ and those who don't yet know Jesus.

> **Demonic forces work tirelessly. Their chief aims are to (1) discredit God's authority, (2) lead humanity away from the paths of righteousness, and (3) disrupt all harmony in the relationship between God and His creation.**

Chapter Four

Demonic Oppression versus Demonic Possession

In the absence of understanding, the concepts of demonic oppression and possession can stir controversy and confusion. Simply put, the terms are interconnected and represent different degrees of spiritual influence by malign spirits. Understanding the distinctions helps to clarify the complex battle between light and darkness. So, let's examine the distinctions between these two spiritual states, from a Christian perspective.

Demonic Oppression

Demonic oppression refers to the external influence of negative spiritual forces upon an individual's life. This oppression encompasses a range of experiences from subtle disturbances to more profound challenges. Demonic oppression can manifest in the various aspects of a person's life and work that impact overall well-being.

Symptoms of demonic oppression include the following:

- Intrusive thoughts, recurring negative emotions, unease, and a sense of heaviness that manifests mentally, spiritually, and physically
- Procrastination, indecision, compromise, confusion, doubt, rationalization, loss of memory, and other common emotional and physical disturbances
- Physical ailments, sleep disturbances, anxiety, or depression
- Addictions, including common addictions to nicotine and alcohol
- Physical infirmities, diseases, and physical afflictions due to spirits of infirmity (Luke 13:11)

All of the symptoms listed above can also be found in people who are demon possessed, perhaps in more severe or dramatic forms. Although we might consider certain symptoms to be demonic because of their negative effects on human beings, not every symptom is a sign of demonic oppression or possession in every case.

Demonic Possession

Demonic possession goes beyond oppression, with negative spiritual entities exerting a profound level of internal control over an individual's mind and body. People suffering from demonic possession may exhibit behaviors, speech patterns, or actions that are inconsistent with their character. As a result, they appear to be overwhelmingly dominated by "outside" forces and increasingly disconnected from their true selves.

Common manifestations of indwelling (possessing) demonic spirits include but are not limited to the following:[1]

- The inability to speak or see; loss of control over one's faculties (Luke 11:14; Matthew 12:22)
- Speaking in a changed voice, as when a demon speaks through the victim (Mark 5:9); outbursts or uncontrolled use of the tongue (lying, cursing, blasphemy, criticism, mockery, railing, and gossip)
- Acts of self-harm (Mark 5:5)
- Unusual strength or ferocity (Luke 8:29; Matthew 8:28)
- Recurring seizures (Mark 9:17–18)
- Severe emotional and mental disturbances that persist or recur, including disturbances

in the mind or thought life (mental torment, procrastination, indecision, compromise, confusion, doubt, rationalization, and loss of memory)
- Addictions, including common addictions to nicotine and alcohol
- Recurring unclean thoughts and acts regarding sex (fantasy sex experiences, masturbation, lust, perversions, homosexuality, fornication, adultery, incest, provocativeness, and harlotry)
- Physical infirmities due to spirits of infirmity (Luke 13:11)

When a spirit of infirmity (whether emotional, mental, or physical) is cast out, there is often the need to pray for healing of whatever damage has occurred. Remember that not every symptom in a list can be automatically attributed to demon possession. Such assumptions can stigmatize people or cause them to avoid getting the medical, psychological, and other care they need.

When demonic possession is involved, intensive spiritual intervention, such as casting the demons out, is necessary for complete deliverance. This undertaking should not be taken lightly. It is a serious form of intervention requiring wisdom and understanding. If you have not been involved in deliverance before, seeking the guidance of spiritual leaders in the know can protect everyone involved and help ensure a good outcome for the person suffering under demonic possession. Working with others is also preferable to working alone, even for experienced ministers.

The terms demonic oppression and demonic possession are interconnected and represent different degrees of spiritual influence by malign spirits.

Chapter Five

Opening Demonic Portals

We know that demons exist and are able to influence people, but how they gain entrance and possess them is a subject all its own. For our purposes, we can address some basic points concerning the nature of spiritual influence and the interaction between the physical and spiritual realms.

Demonic forces are shrewd. They have studied human behavior for millennia and are always looking for someone to exploit. They can use a wide variety of tactics to oppress or possess individuals, but their strategy is always the same: they gain entrance into their victims' lives by what we will call *portals*. These open doors are existing vulnerabilities that demons can prey upon, and they include the conscious and unconscious choices people make.

We don't always open portals on purpose, and how they were opened doesn't matter to demons. As far as they are concerned, every unprotected entry point is an invitation. Demons will use emotional wounds, unresolved traumas, moral weaknesses, uncontrolled attitudes, aberrant relationships, abortion, unforgiveness, drugs, alcohol, fear, sexual addiction, incest, sexual molestation, and other types of access points to their advantage.

Demons are astute where our choices are concerned. They particularly exploit practices or behaviors that align with demonic ways. These can include exploring or participating in occult practices and spiritism involving seances, witchcraft, magic, Ouija boards, levitation, palmistry, ESP, hypnosis, horoscopes, astrology, and divination. Any method of seeking supernatural knowledge, wisdom, guidance, and power apart from God is forbidden. Entertaining or embracing any beliefs that are contrary to God's Word can serve as invitations that demons will eagerly accept.

Sin and Temptation as Portals

Some portals are inadvertent; but sometimes we make overtly sinful choices and then consciously and consistently repeat them. This creates an environment that demons cannot resist. They see it as a wide-open doorway by which they can come and go as they please and accomplish the will of their master, Satan.

Promiscuity is a good example of such a portal. I remember a young man who often attended a church where I was a member. He had many different girlfriends, one of whom was developmentally challenged. Although she was not a child, she was particularly vulnerable to sexual exploitation by opportunistic men. She in fact ended up pregnant but remained unmarried.

Through his promiscuity, the young man in question exposed this young woman to many spiritual and emotional dangers. But he also opened himself to exploitation by demons. When he sat in church services, he coughed in a bizarre way, making a sound like a barking dog. The sound was so real that I turned to see whether a dog had somehow entered the sanctuary. In time, I sensed what was happening: the man's barking was a manifestation of spirits that had gained access because he was running around like a dog in heat, having sexual relations with many people.

Women can be as vulnerable in this area as men are. I remember a young lady who had a spirit of lust. When other believers prayed for her, she would fall out on the floor, gyrating and making sexual noises as though she were having intercourse with an invisible partner. Sometimes, she slithered on the floor like a snake. Her willingness to engage in sin had opened a portal to demonic activity, and spirits traveled through it freely.

Demonic forces also find ways to exploit temptations that entice us toward sinful thoughts and behaviors and away from God's path. Dabbling in occult practices, rituals, or spiritual pursuits outside of God's Word is dangerous. Over time, repeatedly succumbing to such temptations can lead to deeper influence or possession by demons.

Ungodly Religions, Symbols, and Practices

Ungodly religious and cultural symbols and acts can also invite demonic activity. I have done missionary work in Haiti numerous times. When I first arrived at the airport there, I noticed a huge demonic figure or doll-like creature in the form of a balloon that stood more than one hundred feet tall. More recently, that figure has been removed. But I have seen the same image framed and displayed on the walls of four-star, American-style Haitian hotels.

I remember trying to sleep in my hotel room and experiencing nightmares and a variety of spirits in the room. I began to pray and anoint the room. As I prayed in the name of Jesus, all demonic forces had to leave. I reclaimed my temporary dwelling place for God's kingdom. But their influence remained in that hotel because its designers had opened demonic portals by displaying ungodly images.

Involvement in idolatry and any type of religious error can open the door for demonic spirits. Objects and literature can also attract demons. The Scriptures are very clear about avoiding such errors:

> When you come into the land which the Lord your God is giving you, you shall not learn to follow the abominations of those nations. There shall not be found among you anyone who makes his son or his daughter pass through the fire, or one who practices witchcraft, or a soothsayer, or one who interprets omens, or a sorcerer, or one who conjures spells, or a medium, or a spiritist, or one who calls up the dead. For all who do these things are an abomination to the Lord, and because of these abominations the Lord your God drives them out from before you. You shall be blameless before the Lord your God. For these nations which you will dispossess listened to soothsayers and diviners; but as for you, the Lord your God has not appointed such for you. The Lord your God will raise up for you a Prophet like me from your midst, from your brethren. Him you shall hear (Deuteronomy 18:9–15).

False religions (including Eastern religions, philosophies, and mind science), false doctrines, ungodly symbols, and false prophets are invitations to demonic spirits. In his first epistle to Timothy, the apostle Paul warned of a great increase in doctrinal errors promoted by deceiving and seducing spirits in the last days (1 Tim. 4:1). These deceptions deny the inspiration of the Holy Scripture, distract Christians from the move of the Holy Spirit, cause disunity in the body of Christ, and cause confusion in the church through an obsession with doctrines.

Certain sects and cults (such as Mormonism, Jehovah's Witness, Christian Science, Rosicrucianism, and Theosophy) hold to some Christian beliefs but are distorted offshoots of Christianity. Therefore, they are open portals of religious error. Some cults are known as lodges, societies, or social agencies. They create false impressions by using religion, Scripture, and God as their supposed foundations. But they omit the blood atonement of Jesus Christ, which typically reveals cult status.

Demonic portals are easily opened but often harder to close. By keeping our hearts and minds fixed on God and His Word, we can keep demons from trafficking in and out of our lives. David's prayerful words will help us to stay on the righteous path: "Let the words of my mouth and the meditations of my heart be acceptable in Your sight, O Lord, my strength and my Redeemer" (Psalm 19:14).

Demons exploit portals, meaning they cleverly prey on existing vulnerabilities and capitalize on the conscious and unconscious choices we make.

Chapter Six

When Demons Disrupt the Church

Conversations about demonic spirits and deliverance are also about spiritual warfare—a concept involving the belief in an unseen realm where forces of good and evil contend for influence over human lives. Spiritual forces can clash, not only in dark or unseemly places, but even in our church services. Demonic spirits are eager to hinder worship, taint Christian fellowship, and stunt the spiritual growth of believers. In this respect, the local church becomes a battleground.

Demonic activity can take many forms during a church service. All of them are disruptive, but some are less apparent than others. Disruptions can be personal and private, coming through intrusive thoughts, restlessness, sleepiness, and a lack of focus on the message or purpose of the service. Sudden emotional shifts can divert your attention from worship and prayer. An inner resistance can close your heart to the message being preached. You can find yourself torn between the truths of love, hope, and unity and the lies that demons suggest in contradiction to God's Word.

Some demonic manifestations that happen in church are more dramatic. They can include sudden outbursts, erratic movements, and other public behaviors that disturb the worship environment for others. Some are extreme, such as people crawling on the floor, screaming, howling, hissing, and foaming at the mouth. I have witnessed all of these and have seen people beating on the floors or the pews, struggling, fighting, jerking their bodies, laughing out loud, mocking, and crying.

When people become disorderly in church, we need to realize that they are tormented. Some display spirits of pride, control, or lust. Some develop peculiar odors (sometimes linked to diseases such as cancers), and some spontaneously suffer from nausea and pain. Such occurrences seem surprising, but the Bible describes equally disturbing events, including an incident that is recorded in Mark's Gospel:

> Then one of the crowd answered and said, "Teacher, I brought You my son, who has a mute spirit. And wherever it seizes him, it

throws him down; he foams at the mouth, gnashes his teeth, and becomes rigid. So I spoke to Your disciples, that they should cast it out, but they could not" (Mark 9:17–18).

You may have witnessed unusual events at church. Maybe you have seen people projecting their tongues in a snake-like fashion or blowing air through their nostrils and hissing. Maybe you have seen someone's hands become stiff and gnarled or have witnessed an attempted suicide. If you have been in church at least once, you have probably noticed the spirit of pride in people who sit back with their arms folded and their heads tilted back as though to sneer or ignore the service.

Demonic church disturbances come in endless varieties. Whether we choose to realize it or not, they happen often.

Pastoral Approaches to Spiritual Challenges in Church Services

As we saw in Chapter 2, pastors are vital to their congregations. Both their presence and example help to form the church, as individuals and as a body. The pastor and staff are responsible for maintaining an environment that fosters spiritual growth and connection. Some pastors see the removal of disruptive demonic spirits as part of their duty. Therefore, they confront disturbances head-on, not in a belligerent way but by asserting their rightful authority and casting out the demons. Other pastors feel compelled to protect the message they are sharing by ignoring demonic spirits and continuing with the service. They might expect disturbances to resolve themselves without intervention, or they might simply be unsure of how to handle demons.

Many pastors and lay Christians who believe in the existence of demonic entities choose not to engage in casting them out during church services. Some make this choice believing that the casting out of demons is the exclusive practice of other denominations or belief systems. Some avoid casting out demons because they believe it could be divisive or could lead to unnecessary fear or anxiety for their congregations. But are these positions sustainable, and are they helping the church in the long run?

I don't believe that God wants any Christian to be ignorant or powerless. He has called the church to preach the gospel of Jesus Christ, heal the sick, and raise the dead. And notice what Jesus said in Mark's Gospel: "These signs will follow those who believe: In My name *they will cast out demons*; they will speak with new tongues; they will take up serpents; and if they drink anything deadly, it will by no means hurt them;

they will lay hands on the sick, and they will recover" (Mark 16:17–18).

I shared with you the question that prompted me to write this book: I asked myself, "Why aren't pastors casting out demons when they manifest?" I don't pose that question in a disrespectful way. I love and appreciate pastors. They have been a huge part of my life, spiritual growth, and overall well-being. But I believe my question is valid and worthy of an answer. In fact, the larger question is, "Why aren't *we* casting out demons when they manifest?"

Demonic manifestations in church are particularly sensitive, and I agree that protecting the purity of the preached Word is important. I also agree that frightening the congregation is not a pastoral goal. But is it OK to let demons disrupt your church service and interfere with the people's spiritual growth and well-being? I propose that it is not. Whether pastors and others are afraid to make mistakes, look foolish, scare the people, or face demons, fear is the wrong reason not to act. In fact, fear is one of the greatest factors keeping people from fulfilling the Great Commission.

Scripture says that "God has not given us a spirit of fear, but of power and of love and of a sound mind" (2 Timothy 1:7). Whether it's the fear of demons or the fear of looking silly, fear is from the devil himself, and we need to reject it. Jesus said, "Behold, I give you the authority to trample on serpents and scorpions, and over all the power of the enemy, and nothing shall by any means hurt you" (Luke 10:19).

Let's approach demonic disturbances from the position of faith rather than fear, doing what Jesus said to do: use the authority He gave us to cast demons out of our church services and out of our lives.

Spiritual forces can clash, not only in dark or unseemly places, but even in our church services. Demonic spirits are eager to hinder worship, taint Christian fellowship, and stunt the spiritual growth of believers. In this respect, the local church becomes a battleground.

Chapter Seven

Empowered to Cast Out Demons

The process of casting out demons is not based on human ability or power; it is rooted in the belief first and foremost that God has all power and authority over all spiritual realms. Secondly, God gave His only begotten Son, Jesus Christ, all power and authority. Finally, Jesus gave believers power and authority to do the works that He did and even "greater works" that would be possible after His ascension (John 14:12).

If we are Christians, we are empowered to cast out demons. We rely on Jesus' powerful name when we command demonic spirits to come out of those the devil is holding captive. When we counteract negative spiritual influences, we create an atmosphere that is conducive to worship, unity, spiritual growth, and deliverance.

Prepared for Power

Although we as believers are empowered to cast out demons, we are also responsible for living holy, walking in forgiveness, and staying in a state of spiritual preparedness. When we are spiritually attuned and aligned with God's will, we are better equipped with the discernment and wisdom that are critical when casting out demons.

Protecting ourselves against demonic forces involves cultivating a strong relationship with God through prayer, Scripture study, and a lifestyle that reflects our alignment with God's Word. We need to cultivate our preparedness by keeping certain spiritual habits and disciplines—*before* engaging in deliverance ministry and the casting out of demons.

The following habits, disciplines, and scriptures will help you to prepare for such ministry:

- *Affirm your faith in Jesus Christ.* Meditate on Joel 2:32: "It shall come to pass that whoever calls on the name of the Lord shall be saved. For in Mount Zion and in Jerusalem there shall be deliverance, as the Lord has said, among the remnant whom the Lord calls."
- *Confess and repent of any sin in your life.* Meditate on 1 John 1:9: "If we confess our sins, He is

faithful and just to forgive us our sins and to cleanse us from all unrighteousness."

- *Pray and fast.* Meditate on Mark 9:17–29, which involves the healing of a boy with a mute spirit. In Jesus' absence, His disciples tried to heal the boy, with no success. When Jesus returned, His disciples asked Him why they failed. He explained that "this kind [of spirit] can come out by nothing but prayer and fasting" (Mark 9:29).
- *Look only to Jesus, our Deliverer.* Meditate on 2 Samuel 22:2: "The Lord is my rock and my fortress and my deliverer."
- *Forgive every person who has ever harmed or wronged you.* Meditate on Matthew 6:14–15: "If you forgive men their trespasses, your heavenly Father will also forgive you. But if you do not forgive men their trespasses, neither will your Father forgive your trespasses."
- *Break ties with any false religion, all witchcraft, and all forms of the occult.* Meditate on Deuteronomy 18:10–11: "There shall not be found among you anyone who makes his son or his daughter pass through the fire, or one who practices witchcraft, or a soothsayer, or one who interprets omens, or a sorcerer, or one who conjures spells, or a medium, or a spiritist, or one who calls up the dead."

- *Have a pure and clean heart.* Meditate on Matthew 5:8 "Blessed are the pure in heart, for they shall see God."

Dressed to Serve

Preparing your heart so you can be a ready vessel is essential. But you also need to dress for the occasion. According to the Scriptures, we are to remain clothed in God's armor, which the apostle Paul describes in his letter to the church at Ephesus:

> Finally, my brethren, be strong in the Lord and in the power of His might. Put on the whole armor of God, that you may be able to stand against the wiles of the devil. For we do not wrestle against flesh and blood, but against principalities, against powers, against the rulers of the darkness of this age, against spiritual hosts of wickedness in the heavenly places. Therefore take up the whole armor of God, that you may be able to withstand in the evil day, and having done all, to stand. Stand therefore, having girded your waist with truth, having put on the breastplate of righteousness, and having shod your feet with the preparation of the gospel of peace; above all, taking the shield of faith with which you will be able to quench all the fiery darts of the

> wicked one. And take the helmet of salvation, and the sword of the Spirit, which is the word of God; praying always with all prayer and supplication in the Spirit, being watchful to this end with all perseverance and supplication for all the saints (Ephesians 6:10–18).

Paul emphasized the importance of being spiritually prepared and protected. He minced no words when naming the principalities, powers, rulers of the darkness of this age, and spiritual hosts of wickedness in the heavenly places. Yet, many (if not most) people—*including many Christians*—remain unaware of demonic spirits, not realizing that their ignorance and fear have invited demonic activity and its destructive effects.

Avoiding spiritual realities leaves us defenseless in ministry and leaves untold numbers of people under the power of demonic forces. Without deliverance, they will continue to endure whatever torments the devil inflicts on them. To varying degrees, their mental, emotional, and physical pain keep them as mercilessly imprisoned as if they were surrounded by steel bars.

If you have been called by God to the ministry of the gospel, you will meet (and probably already have met) people who desperately need deliverance. Will you ignore their need and disregard the demons that are afflicting them? Or will you become part of the solution God has already prepared for them, and for you as His vessel? The choice is clear, and it is yours.

> **Jesus gave believers power and authority to do the works that He did and even "greater works" that would be possible after His ascension (John 14:12).**

Chapter Eight

Following Jesus, Our Exemplar

During His earthly ministry, Jesus interacted with demonic forces and embodied His role as the ultimate conqueror of darkness. (See Luke 8:1–3, 26–37, and 11:14–23; Matthew 17:14–21. See also the Appendix.). His authority, compassion, and teachings reveal powerful ways of navigating the spiritual realm, standing firm in faith, and embracing the redemption and victory that Jesus purchased for all who are indwelled by His Spirit and obedient to His Word.

Jesus' purpose then and now is to set at liberty everyone who is being held captive by the devil. We are to lead these people to the relief that only Christ can give. Therefore, we must train and teach deliverance from generation to generation. Most importantly, we need to follow what Jesus did. Whatever kind of spirit He confronted—whether it was a deaf and dumb spirit, a spirit of lust, a spirit of sickness, etc.—Jesus commanded it to come out. And so should we!

We are called to command demonic spirits to leave, in Jesus' name, remembering that the Spirit of the living God is within us. Yes! The same Spirit that raised Jesus Christ from the dead *dwells within us*. Therefore, we have authority over demons. When we command them to come out of someone, they must come out and bow their knee to the name of Jesus, who is the living Word of God.

When Someone Manifests a Demonic Spirit

Casting out demons is a scriptural activity that restores people who have been afflicted by unclean spirits. It also demonstrates two key truths in the life of faith:

1. The existence of two opposing spiritual kingdoms
2. The victory of God's kingdom over Satan's

Being involved in or witnessing a deliverance is an unforgettable experience and an essential part of the Christian faith. However, it is one thing to believe that God's power works within you to accomplish His will;

it is another to actually operate in that power. You and I are called to rise to the occasion when demonic activity manifests in our presence. The following are simple suggestions to follow when you minister to someone who is under some sort of demonic influence:

- Remember that you are dealing with a unique human being. Don't assume that you understand the person's situation. Ask questions, such as *Have you been involved in witchcraft? Have you used the Ouija board? Are you involved with a cult or other ungodly form of religion?* As they answer, look to the Holy Spirit for discernment and guidance.
- If the person confesses ungodly entanglements, such as black magic, white magic, idol worship, etc., ask them to denounce them all, in the name of Jesus.
- Based on what you have heard from the person and from the Holy Spirit, look the person in the eye and command the demon to come out, in the name of Jesus.
- Be prepared. Unpleasant manifestations might occur when you command demons to come out. Stand firm until any manifestations pass and any demons flee. Bear in mind that God breathed into Adam the breath of life (Genesis 2:7). It is not

surprising, therefore, that demons are generally released through the mouth and nose, because spirits are associated with breathing. You might witness, as I have, strange sounds or foaming from the mouth as demons leave.

- Lead the person into a prayer of receiving Jesus Christ as their Lord and Savior.
- Ask the Holy Spirit to come and dwell within the person. Expect the person to get baptized in the Holy Ghost with the evidence of speaking in tongues. Let the person know how important it is to be baptized in water.
- Pray over the person for God's wisdom and for the Holy Spirit to seal the work of deliverance.

Hindrances to Deliverance

Not everyone who is afflicted by demons is ready to be free. A variety of issues can hinder a person's ability to receive much-needed deliverance:

- A lack of repentance for sin (Revelation 3:19)
- A refusal to break agreement with demonic spirits (Amos 3:3)
- The failure to forgive others (Mark 11:25–26)
- An unwillingness to confess one's sins (James 5:16)

Allow the Holy Spirit to minister to people who are struggling with any hindrances. Let Him give you wisdom for the situation and help you to share the path to freedom.

Helping People Maintain Their Deliverance

Only God can deliver people from demonic influence. Because demons will try to return, deliverance needs to be maintained. You can help people by urging them to do the following:

- Make Jesus Christ the Lord of their lives (John 12:31–32; Rom. 10:9–10).
- Attend church services and study the Bible regularly (Hebrews 10:24–25; 2 Timothy 3:15–17).
- Testify of their deliverance (Revelation 12:11).
- Once their spiritual lives are "swept clean" through deliverance, they must leave no empty spaces or the demon that was cast out will take "with him seven other spirits more wicked than himself, and they [will return to] enter and dwell there" (Matthew 12:43–45).
- Stay filled with the Holy Spirit (Ephesians 5:18).

- Put on the whole armor of God (Ephesians 6:10–18).
- Be obedient to God and resist the devil (James 4:7).
- Keep themselves in the love of God (Jude 20–21).
- Entertain only godly thoughts (Phil. 4:8).
- Cultivate godly relationships (Hebrews 10:25; 1 Thessalonians 5:11).

Jesus has empowered you to follow His example in all aspects of your life. When you minister to the oppressed in His name, trust Him to lead you by His Spirit and accomplish His will in and through you. He is more than willing to do it—He is waiting to do it!

We can follow Jesus' example because the Spirit of the living God is within us. Yes! The same Spirit that raised Jesus Christ from the dead dwells within us.

Afterword

Power, Authority, Compassion, and Healing

The life and teachings of Jesus Christ stand as a beacon illuminating the path of faith, compassion, and wisdom. As the Son of God and Son of Man, His power and authority framed His approach to demonic spirits. Coming as God in the flesh, He demonstrated unparalleled power over all spiritual realms, asserting control and commanding even the most wicked entities to submit.

Motivated by compassion and the desire to bring healing and deliverance to those in spiritual bondage, Jesus confronted demons head-on and commanded them to leave those they had tormented (see the Appendix). These encounters reveal His power to liberate people from spiritual chains and demonstrate the triumph of light over darkness.

Afterword

Casting Out Demons in the New Testament

The four Gospels show that deliverance and the casting out of demons were integral to Jesus' earthly ministry. Because we are called to follow His example and are commissioned to go in His name, His works are integral to our callings. Therefore, we will consider several Scripture passages that capture the essence of Jesus' ministry and His approach in serving God and humankind. The first is a passage from Acts that provides context about Jesus Himself:

> The word which God sent to the children of Israel, preaching peace through Jesus Christ—He is Lord of all—that word you know, which was proclaimed throughout all Judea, and began from Galilee after the baptism which John preached: how God anointed Jesus of Nazareth with the Holy Spirit and with power, who went about doing good and healing all who were oppressed by the devil, for God was with Him (Acts 10:36–38).

The New Testament presents several of Jesus Christ's encounters involving demonic oppression or possession. Please read the following accounts as though for the first time. Let them heighten your sense of all that Jesus did and all that is possible in His name.

Afterword

Jesus went about all Galilee, teaching in their synagogues, preaching the gospel of the kingdom, and healing all kinds of sickness and all kinds of disease among the people. Then His fame went throughout all Syria; and they brought to Him all sick people who were afflicted with various diseases and torments, and those who were demon-possessed, epileptics, and paralytics; and He healed them. Great multitudes followed Him—from Galilee, and from Decapolis, Jerusalem, Judea, and beyond the Jordan (Matthew 4:23–25).

When [Jesus] had come out of the boat, immediately there met Him out of the tombs a man with an unclean spirit, who had his dwelling among the tombs; and no one could bind him, not even with chains, because he had often been bound with shackles and chains. And the chains had been pulled apart by him, and the shackles broken in pieces; neither could anyone tame him. And always, night and day, he was in the mountains and in the tombs, crying out and cutting himself with stones.
When he saw Jesus from afar, he ran and worshiped Him. And he cried out with a loud voice and said, "What have I to do with You,

Afterword

Jesus, Son of the Most High God? I implore You by God that You do not torment me."
For He said to him, "Come out of the man, unclean spirit!" Then He asked him, "What is your name?"
And he answered, saying, "My name is Legion; for we are many." Also he begged Him earnestly that He would not send them out of the country.
Now a large herd of swine was feeding there near the mountains. So all the demons begged Him, saying, "Send us to the swine, that we may enter them." And at once Jesus gave them permission. Then the unclean spirits went out and entered the swine (there were about two thousand); and the herd ran violently down the steep place into the sea, and drowned in the sea.
So those who fed the swine fled, and they told it in the city and in the country. And they went out to see what it was that had happened. Then they came to Jesus, and saw the one who had been demon-possessed and had the legion, sitting and clothed and in his right mind. And they were afraid. And those who saw it told them how it happened to him who had been demon-possessed, and about the swine (Mark 5:2–16).

Afterword

Then [Jesus] went down to Capernaum, a city of Galilee, and was teaching them on the Sabbaths. And they were astonished at His teaching, for His word was with authority. Now in the synagogue there was a man who had a spirit of an unclean demon. And he cried out with a loud voice, saying, "Let us alone! What have we to do with You, Jesus of Nazareth? Did You come to destroy us? I know who You are—the Holy One of God!" But Jesus rebuked him, saying, "Be quiet, and come out of him!" And when the demon had thrown him in their midst, it came out of him and did not hurt him. Then they were all amazed and spoke among themselves, saying, "What a word this is! For with authority and power He commands the unclean spirits, and they come out" (Luke 4:31–36).

Then one of the crowd answered and said, "Teacher, I brought You my son, who has a mute spirit. And wherever it seizes him, it throws him down; he foams at the mouth, gnashes his teeth, and becomes rigid. So I spoke to Your disciples, that they should cast it out, but they could not." He answered him and said, "O faithless generation, how long shall I be with you? How long shall I bear with you? Bring him to Me." Then they brought him to Him. And when he saw Him, immediately the spirit convulsed him, and he fell on the ground and wallowed, foaming at the mouth.

So He asked his father, "How long has this been happening to him?"

And he said, "From childhood. And often he has thrown him both into the fire and into the water to destroy him. But if You can do anything, have compassion on us and help us."

Jesus said to him, "If you can believe, all things are possible to him who believes."

Immediately the father of the child cried out and said with tears, "Lord, I believe; help my unbelief!"

When Jesus saw that the people came running together, He rebuked the unclean spirit, saying to it, "Deaf and dumb spirit, I command you, come out of him and enter him no more!"

Then the spirit cried out, convulsed him greatly, and came out of him. And he became as one dead, so that many said, "He is dead." But Jesus took him by the hand and lifted him up, and he arose.

And when He had come into the house, His disciples asked Him privately, "Why could we not cast it out?"

So He said to them, "This kind can come out

by nothing but prayer and fasting" (Mark 9:17–29).

These passages are powerful and instructive! Yet John's Gospel tells us that "there are also many other things that Jesus did, which if they were written one by one ... even the world itself could not contain the books that would be written. Amen" (John 21:25).

Jesus Is Tempted by Satan

Scripture also describes an encounter between Jesus and Satan. After Jesus was baptized in the Jordan, the Holy Spirit led Him into the wilderness, where he fasted for forty days. Matthew 4:1–11 describes the encounter and highlights Jesus' complete triumph over the devil and his schemes. Satan tried to divert Jesus from His divine mission, but Jesus responded with an unwavering commitment to God's will, solidifying His role as the ultimate conqueror of darkness.

> Then Jesus was led up by the Spirit into the wilderness to be tempted by the devil. And when He had fasted forty days and forty nights, afterward He was hungry. Now when the tempter came to Him, he said, "If You are the Son of God, command that these stones become bread."
> But He answered and said, "It is written, 'Man

Afterword

shall not live by bread alone, but by every word that proceeds from the mouth of God.'"
Then the devil took Him up into the holy city, set Him on the pinnacle of the temple, and said to Him, "If You are the Son of God, throw Yourself down. For it is written: 'He shall give His angels charge over you,' and, 'In their hands they shall bear you up, Lest you dash your foot against a stone.'"
Jesus said to him, "It is written again, 'You shall not tempt the Lord your God.'"
Again, the devil took Him up on an exceedingly high mountain, and showed Him all the kingdoms of the world and their glory. And he said to Him, "All these things I will give You if You will fall down and worship me."
Then Jesus said to him, "Away with you, Satan! For it is written, 'You shall worship the Lord your God, and Him only you shall serve.'"
Then the devil left Him, and behold, angels came and ministered to Him (Matthew 4:1–11).

Matthew's account of this important confrontation shows how Jesus responded to the devil and crushed each satanic attempt to control Him. Jesus discerned the situation perfectly and exercised His authority

Afterword

with precision, thoroughly dismantling the devil's agenda.

During His earthly walk, Jesus shared His knowledge and wisdom with His disciples and gave them explicit instructions on how to resist the devil. Matthew 10:1 says that "when He had called His twelve disciples to Him, He gave them power over unclean spirits, to cast them out, and to heal all kinds of sickness and all kinds of disease." He granted this authority for kingdom purposes. He gave His disciples further instruction in Acts 1:8, saying, "You shall receive power when the Holy Spirit has come upon you; and you shall be witnesses to Me in Jerusalem, and in all Judea and Samaria, and to the end of the earth."

God did not create us to be powerless, whether we are in the pews or the pulpit. We should not need to ask why demons aren't being cast out. The church should be casting out demons whenever they manifest. This task is not only for pastors but for every believer who names Jesus as Lord. And if we don't do it, who will?

Through His ministry, Jesus commanded us as believers to follow in His footsteps, always relying on prayer, faith, fasting, and the power of God's Word. Through His death, resurrection, and ascension, He made it possible for us to complete every divine assignment. His triumph over darkness testifies to the redemptive power of His sacrifice and offers hope,

Afterword

freedom, and salvation to all who believe in Him. His example underscores…

- the importance of relying on God's Word;
- the power and authority given to us as believers;
- the sacred embrace of compassion;
- the call to stand firm in faith when confronting the forces of darkness.

Jesus Christ's encounters with Satan and with demonic spirits reveal Him as the eternal victor over all wicked spirits and influences. His triumph over darkness reminds us that through Him, we can overcome wickedness, temptations, and all the challenges of this life. We can experience the transforming power of God. And through Him, we can help others to experience the same.

Motivated by compassion and a desire to bring healing and deliverance to those in spiritual bondage, Jesus confronted demons head-on. These encounters reveal His power to liberate people from spiritual chains and demonstrate the triumph of light over darkness.

Appendix

Satan and Demons in Scripture

Each of the scriptures below mentions demons and/or unclean or evil spirits. As a refresher, read them as they are listed here. Or for a deeper understanding, read them in their larger contexts. Let the Word of God instruct and encourage you in your role as you follow Christ.

Matthew 4:24: Then His fame went throughout all Syria; and they brought to Him all sick people who were afflicted with various diseases and torments, and those who were demon-possessed, epileptics, and paralytics; and He healed them.

Matthew 8:16: When evening had come, they brought to Him many who were demon-possessed.

And He cast out the spirits with a word, and healed all who were sick.

Matthew 8:28–33: When He had come to the other side, to the country of the Gergesenes, there met Him two demon-possessed men, coming out of the tombs, exceedingly fierce, so that no one could pass that way. And suddenly they cried out, saying, "What have we to do with You, Jesus, You Son of God? Have You come here to torment us before the time? Now a good way off from them there was a herd of many swine feeding. So the demons begged Him, saying, "If You cast us out, permit us to go away into the herd of swine." And He said to them, "Go." So when they had come out, they went into the herd of swine. And suddenly the whole herd of swine ran violently down the steep place into the sea, and perished in the water. Then those who kept them fled; and they went away into the city and told everything, including what had happened to the demon-possessed men.

Matthew 9:32–33: As they went out, behold, they brought to Him a man, mute and demon-possessed. And when the demon was cast out, the mute spoke. And the multitudes marveled, saying, "It was never seen like this in Israel!"

Appendix

Matthew 10:8: Heal the sick, cleanse the lepers, raise the dead, cast out demons. Freely you have received, freely give.

Matthew 12:22: Then one was brought to Him who was demon-possessed, blind and mute; and He healed him, so that the blind and mute man both spoke and saw.

Matthew 12:28: If I [Jesus] cast out demons by the Spirit of God, surely the kingdom of God has come upon you.

Mark 1:32–34: At evening, when the sun had set, they brought to Him all who were sick and those who were demon-possessed. And the whole city was gathered together at the door. Then He healed many who were sick with various diseases, and cast out many demons; and He did not allow the demons to speak, because they knew Him.

Mark 1:39: [Jesus] was preaching in their synagogues throughout all Galilee, and casting out demons.

Mark 3:14–15: Then He appointed twelve, that they might be with Him and that He might send them out to preach, and to have power to heal sicknesses and to cast out demons.

Mark 6:13: They cast out many demons, and anointed with oil many who were sick, and healed them.

Mark 16:9: When He rose early on the first day of the week, He appeared first to Mary Magdalene, out of whom He had cast seven demons.

Mark 16:17: These signs will follow those who believe: In My name they will cast out demons; they will speak with new tongues.

Luke 4:41: Demons also came out of many, crying out and saying, "You are the Christ, the Son of God!" And He, rebuking them, did not allow them to speak, for they knew that He was the Christ.

Luke 8:1–2: The twelve were with Him, and certain women who had been healed of evil spirits and infirmities—Mary called Magdalene, out of whom had come seven demons.

Luke 8:27–36: When He stepped out on the land, there met Him a certain man from the city who had demons for a long time. And he wore no clothes, nor did he live in a house but in the tombs. When he saw Jesus, he cried out, fell down before Him, and with a loud voice said, "What have I to do with You, Jesus, Son of the Most High God? I beg You, do not torment me!" For He had commanded the unclean spirit to come out of the man. For it had often seized him, and he was kept under guard, bound with chains and shackles; and he broke the bonds and was driven by the demon into the wilderness. Jesus asked him, saying, "What is your name?" And he said, "Legion," because many demons had entered him. And they begged Him that He would not command them to go out into the abyss. Now a herd of many swine was feeding there on the mountain. So they begged Him that He would permit them to enter them. And He permitted them. Then the demons went out of the man and entered the swine, and the herd ran violently down the steep place into the lake and drowned. When those who fed them saw what had happened, they fled and told it in the city and in the country. Then they went out to see what had happened, and came to Jesus, and found the man from whom the demons had departed, sitting at the feet of Jesus, clothed and in his right mind. And they were afraid. They also who had seen it told them by what means he who had been demon-possessed was healed.

Luke 9:1: Then He called His twelve disciples together and gave them power and authority over all demons, and to cure diseases.

Luke 10:17: Then the seventy returned with joy, saying, "Lord, even the demons are subject to us in Your name."

Luke 11:14: [Jesus] was casting out a demon, and it was mute. So it was, when the demon had gone out, that the mute spoke; and the multitudes marveled.

Luke 11:18–20: If Satan also is divided against himself, how will his kingdom stand? Because you say I cast out demons by Beelzebub. And if I [Jesus] cast out demons by Beelzebub, by whom do your sons cast them out? Therefore they will be your judges. But if I cast out demons with the finger of God, surely the kingdom of God has come upon you.

Luke 13:32: [Jesus] said to them, "Go, tell that fox, 'Behold, I cast out demons and perform cures today and tomorrow, and the third day I shall be perfected.'"

Acts 8:7–8: Unclean spirits, crying with a loud voice, came out of many who were possessed; and many who were paralyzed and lame were healed. And there was great joy in that city.

Acts 19:13–17: Then some of the itinerant Jewish exorcists took it upon themselves to call the name of the Lord Jesus over those who had evil spirits, saying,

Appendix

"We exorcise you by the Jesus whom Paul preaches." Also there were seven sons of Sceva, a Jewish chief priest, who did so. And the evil spirit answered and said, "Jesus I know, and Paul I know; but who are you?" Then the man in whom the evil spirit was leaped on them, overpowered them, and prevailed against them, so that they fled out of that house naked and wounded. This became known both to all Jews and Greeks dwelling in Ephesus; and fear fell on them all, and the name of the Lord Jesus was magnified.

1 Corinthians 10:21: You cannot drink the cup of the Lord and the cup of demons; you cannot partake of the Lord's table and of the table of demons.

James 2:19: You believe that there is one God. You do well. Even the demons believe—and tremble!

Notes

Chapter 3

1. Don Stewart, "Where Did Demons Originate?" Blue Letter Bible, accessed February 26, 2024, https://www.blueletterbible.org/faq/don_stewart/don_stewart_51.cfm.
2. See Hope Bolinger, "What Is a Succubus? Definition and Bible Meaning," Christianity.com, September 25, 2023, https://www.christianity.com/wiki/angels-and-demons/succubus-bible.html.
3. Ibid.
4. "Rabshakeh," Bible Study Tools, accessed February 26, 2024, https://www.biblestudytools.com/dictionary/rabshakeh/.
5. Richard T. Ritenbaugh, "What the Bibles Says about Pharmakeia," BibleTools, accessed March 5, 2024, https://www.bibletools.org/index.cfm/fuseaction/Topical.show/RTD/cgg/ID/2945/Pharmakeia.htm.
6. See Bane, *Encyclopedia of Demons*, 76.
7. Ibid.

Chapter 4

1. Thomas Sappington, "Demon Possession," The Gospel Coalition, accessed February 27, 2024, https://www.thegospelcoalition.org/essay/demon-possession/; Don Stewart, "What Happens When a Person Is Demon-Possessed?" Blue Letter Bible, accessed February 27, 2024, https://www.blueletterbible.org/faq/don_stewart/don_stewart_59.cfm.

About the Author

Evangelist Carolyn Walker is a minister of the gospel and a missionary. She has served in various countries including Haiti, Mexico, Santo Domingo, Honduras, Albania, Jamaica, Hong Kong, Singapore, and the  Bahamas. She has been instrumental in building churches in Central America and financially supports the feeding of hundreds of children a day in Copan, Honduras.

From 2002 to 2008, Pastor Carolyn was co-founder and associate pastor of Word of Faith Ministries in Sanford, Florida. After twenty years of service as an officer in the United States Air Force, she served as a pastor on staff at megachurches in Denver, Colorado and Orlando, Florida.

Carolyn loves to hear feedback from readers:
carolynwalks@yahoo.com

www.ingramcontent.com/pod-product-compliance
Lightning Source LLC
LaVergne TN
LVHW041550070426
835507LV00011B/1017